AF413349

TO:
RYAN AND POPPY
I LOVE YOU! ♥

A Day with DAISY

Learn 10 Strategies from a Speech Language Pathologist to Promote your Child's Language Development WHILE Reading to your Child!

Alexandra Princiotta Lowe, MA CCC-SLP

Illustrated by: **Febriyana Fadillah**

Table of Contents

Introduction

The little girl in this story, Daisy, is 2-years-old and only says a handful of words. Typically, 2-year-olds produce 200-400 words and are starting to speak in 2-word phrases. Daisy's parents use strategies they learned from their speech language pathologist AND, as you'll see, the strategies are easily embedded into daily routines.

The author of this story, a licensed and experienced pediatric speech language pathologist, has had great success using these strategies with children ages 0-3 years old for over a decade. These simple tips and tricks can be used with children who are language delayed, like Daisy, children on the Autism Spectrum, and late talkers. There are 10 strategies that will be used throughout the book. This book is not to replace speech therapy, but to act as a tool for your family in conjunction with speech therapy.

How to Use this Book

This book is to be used as a reference and tool for parents, caregivers, and educators. Come back to this book until you can incorporate all 10 strategies without even thinking about it. That's the point! These language tips and tricks should be easily embedded into your daily routines so as you go about your busy lives, you are simultaneously promoting your child's language development.

Go through the 10 strategies or skip ahead to the story. It's up to you! At some point, review the 10 strategies. You will find the examples of the language tips throughout the book. You can also use these strategies with typically developing children to support their language development.

Speech & Language Strategies

1. **Verbal Routines** are short, repetitive phrases that can be used throughout the day in different contexts. Children anticipate that something is going to happen after the repetitive phrase they are used to hearing ('1, 2, 3' or 'ready, set, go') and therefore, will attend to what you are saying. Pause before the last word to give them an opportunity to chime in! Examples on pages 15, 21, 22, 28..

2. **Give Choices!** Children with language delays often feel frustrated. Offering choices can help your little one feel more in control and therefore regulated (calm and ok!). By giving choices, we are constantly labeling items in their environment, which is important for receptive (understanding) language. Children must understand language before they use language expressively. Example: "Do you want your dinosaur bib or your bib with the flowers?" Be sure to hold up both objects in front of your child, that way even if they are not yet speaking, this can prompt them to point. Examples on pages 13, 30

3. **Repeat, repeat, repeat!** Children learn language by hearing a word many times in different contexts. Children who are language delayed often need to hear a word many, MANY times for it to truly "stick." Repetition is key! Instead of talking in long sentences during play, choose a few key words you will target and repeat them as many times as you can! Example: "You are going UP the stairs! Up! Up! Up! We're going... up!" Examples on pages 14, 25.

4. Talk about what YOU are doing. The more language exposure the better! A study done by Professor Anne Fernald of Stanford, found that 2-year-olds who were exposed to less talk had smaller vocabularies and processed language at a slower rate than their peers who heard more words per day (Fernald, 2013). Example: "I'm putting on my shoes because we are going outside!" Examples on pages 11, 16.

5. Pause and Wait! While it is true that the more words your child hears the better, it's also important that they are given the opportunity to talk. By pausing and waiting, you are giving your child a chance to respond, thus teaching "turn taking," which is fundamental for speech and language development. Make a comment or two, and then pause and wait with a smile! Be sure to respond to whatever it is your child did/said to promote turn taking. Try to elicit as many 'back and forth' interactions as you can! Games that teach turn taking are great for demonstrating this; like 'peekaboo,' for babies, and rolling a ball back and forth with your toddler. Examples on pages 12, 17, 18, 26.

6. Parallel Talk. Talk about what YOUR CHILD is doing. Again, be sure to pause so they have an opportunity to speak as well. With parallel talk, you are making comments (not asking questions). We tend to ask our kiddos a lot of questions. For children that are not talking yet or are language delayed, this is confusing! Instead, narrate what your child is doing. It's ok (in fact, encouraged!) to have moments of silence in between comments. Example: "You are putting the block on top. You are making a tower!" Examples on pages 18, 29.

7. Give commands to your little one. Improving their expressive language (talking) is impossible without working on their receptive language (understanding words and their meaning). Typically, 1-year-olds can follow 1-step directions and 2-year-olds can follow 2-step directions. In our busy lives, sometimes it's easier to do everything for our little ones, but they learn language and how to be independent by following simple steps. Toddlers feel a sense of satisfaction when they have completed a task, so give them something to do! This can also help with behavior and self-regulation. Ask your toddler to get their shoes instead of getting them yourself. Have them throw something out in the garbage after each meal. *Examples on pages 15, 16.*

8. **Language Expansion.** Add one to three words to what your child says. If your child says, "car," you can respond with, "Cars go beep beep!" or "Blue car!" *Examples on pages 19, 20, 29.*

9. **Exclamatory words are most certainly words!** These are words like: "uh oh," "yay," "wee," "yum," and "wow!" To encourage your child to produce exclamatory words, use your facial expressions to exaggerate. Gasping before saying an exclamatory word will help get your child's attention. It's important to have their attention so their brains can take in the information. Exclamatory words are great words to target if your child is not talking that much yet. Look at a beautiful sunset together and say, "wow!" in a slow, exaggerated manner. Think about stretching your vowels and talking in a 'sing song' way when using the strategies. *Examples on pages 22, 23.*

10. **Sing/Read & Pause!** Sing familiar songs with your little one and pause before a word. Continue to sing and pause EVEN if your child does not fill in the words right away. Chances are they will at least pause and look at you- now that you have their attention, say the word. In our electronic world it can be easy to just ask Alexa to play a song, but by singing OURSELVES we can slow down the rate, pause, sing and connect as a family! "Twinkle, twinkle little..." The same goes for reading a familiar story. *Examples on pages 24, 31.*

Strategy #4 **Talk about what YOU are doing**

Is your child using gestures? If they are not speaking at all, teaching gestures is a great place to start. Model waving hello and goodbye every chance you get. You can encourage your child to use more gestures by doing so yourself! "More," "open," and "please" are signs in American Sign Language that can also be useful to teach to your little one.

Strategy #5 **Pause & Wait!**

Strategy #2 **Give Choices**

Pointing is a prerequisite for speech and language. Encourage your child to point by holding objects out in front of them instead of giving the object to them straight away. Model pointing yourself when you are on a walk and say, "Look, an airplane!"

Strategy #3 Repeat, repeat, repeat!

Strategy #1 **Verbal Routines**

Strategy #7 **Give Commands**

It may seem silly to constantly narrate what you are doing, but by doing so you are providing your child with a language rich environment! Remember to pause in between your comments to give your child an opportunity to respond.

*Quick tip on how you can prevent picky eating: Instead of asking, "Do you like it," or "Is it yummy," throughout mealtime, use neutral, descriptive language like 'juicy,' and 'crunchy.' This is also great for expanding your child's vocabulary.

**You'll notice that Daisy said, "kwunchie," instead of "crunchy." This is a-ok! We are not concerned with articulation at this stage of speech development. Just be sure to model correct speech (speech without articulation errors).

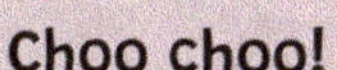

The train goes fast! The train stops!
You are pushing the train.

The train goes...

Choo choo!

Strategy #6 Parallel Talk

Strategy #5 Pause & Wait!

Strategy #8 **Language Expansion**

A note about colors: If your child is language delayed, spend less time focusing on numbers and colors, and target words that have more communicational intent, like, "no," "more," "mine," as well as verbs and nouns. You'll see that Daisy's dad said, "red bike." That's ok! Just don't *only* teach colors.

Strategy #1 **Verbal Routines**

Strategy #1 Verbal Routines

Strategy #9 Exclamatory Words

21

Quick tip: Every time you drop something, say, "uh oh!" Imitation is one of the building blocks for speech and language and it starts with gestures and facial expressions. Be as theatrical and as fun as you'd like! Speaking of imitation, after you take a sip of your drink, let out a refreshing, 'ah' sound!

Rain, rain, go...
Away!
Come again another...
Day!

Strategy #3 **Repeat, repeat, repeat!**

My feet are wet!
My toes are...
Wet!
Strategy #5 Pause & Wait!

Did you know that when your child lifts her arms to be picked up this counts as a gesture? Remember: gestures are communication! Help your child pair their gestures with words by responding to and saying out loud what they are gesturing.

Daisy's mom does not pick her up right away; she uses a verbal routine and waits for her to respond. It's important to teach children that language is reciprocal, meaning they request/say/ or do something, then something else happens. (This is not to say that we should give children everything they request!)

Strategy #8 **Language Expansion**

Strategy #6 **Parallel Talk**

Strategy #2 **Give Choices**

29

Strategy #10 Sing/Read + Pause

Ever notice your little one wants to read the same book over and over? That's great! It's wonderful for their brains to hear the same stories repeatedly because they can anticipate what comes next, which helps develop logical thinking. It is satisfying for children when their predictions are correct.

Another note about reading: Sometimes when little ones are feeling a bit more energetic it is harder for them to sit and listen to an entire story. That's ok! Instead of worrying about reading every word, point to what's on the page and talk about the pictures. Your child will most likely imitate you pointing, which is great since imitation is vital for language! Point to a bird and say, "tweet tweet." Point to the clouds and repeat, "cloud, cloud, cloud" in a fun, slow, sing-songy voice.

A Note to Parents/ Caregivers

This book is not to replace a speech evaluation or speech therapy, but to act as a useful resource. Reach out to your pediatrician if you are concerned with your child's speech and language development. You can also reach out to your state's early intervention services. In many states, a speech language evaluation and speech therapy are at no cost to the family. If your pediatrician tells you to wait to see if your child 'catches up,' I would seek advice from a licensed speech language pathologist. Current research shows us that the brain is malleable, meaning we can truly shape our children's brains by creating new neural pathways, especially from birth to 3-years-old, therefore the earlier the intervention, the better!

Remember that the strategies you have learned from this book are meant to be embedded into your daily routines. They should not feel forced. If you are feeling overwhelmed by the strategies, just pick 1 or 2 to do in certain environments, like bath time or on a walk. Connect with your child and enjoy your time together, engaging in back-and-forth interactions throughout the day. The fact that you have this book shows that you are already doing your best to promote your child's language development!

Notes/ Resources

Anne Fernald's elegant study: Anne Fernald, Virginia A. Marchman, and Adriana Weisleder, "SES differences in language processing skill and vocabulary are evident at 18 months," *Developmental Science* 16.2 (2013): 234-248.

Mize, L. (2011). *Teach me to talk: The therapy manual; a comprehensive guide for treating receptive and expressive language delays and disorders in toddlers and young preschoolers.* Teachmetotalk.com.

Speech & Language Milestones

https://www.cdc.gov/ncbddd/actearly/milestones/milestones-in-action.html

https://www.nidcd.nih.gov/health/speech-and-language

About the Author

Alexandra Princiotta Lowe is a licensed speech language pathologist with her own private practice. She has a passion for helping families feel confident in providing language rich environments for their children. Alex works with children of all ages in both California and New York- thanks to telehealth! She also works with people with aphasia.

Alex lives in Los Angeles, California, with her husband, and daughter, Penelope (Poppy). You might find Alex reading a book on the beach in Fire Island, New York, or hiking with her family in California. Follow her on Instagram - @akp_speechtherapy!

www.akpspeech.com